CAPITOL
ministries®

# Rebuilding America

~

## The Biblical Blueprint

# Praise for Rebuilding America

In the first century church the Great Commission was fulfilled without much in the way of resources or technology. Today we have plenty of both, but the Great Commission remains unfulfilled. Why? Could it be one of strategy and emphasis? This book looks at that factor in great detail. Emphasizing reaching political leaders for Christ was something they did then that we don't do now. This book makes the case for that. A must read for those interested not only in missions, but in changing the direction of a nation.

**US SENATOR STEVE DAINES**
Montana

The church often ignores its key task to speak the love of Christ to a world in desperate need. Ralph Drollinger challenges the church do first things first, which he defends Biblically to mean sharing God's love with leaders. Most of the Old Testament was written to political leaders, by political leaders, or about political leaders. Paul's mission took him to capitals all over the known world. Prophets throughout the Bible challenge leaders to righteousness. God cares about leaders and how their leadership affects people; maybe it is time we start to care about God's work with leaders as well. Ralph Drollinger lays out the Biblical path for those who want to follow Christ as you mentor leaders.

**US SENATOR JAMES LANKFORD**
Oklahoma

When City Council Members are strong in Christ, the course of our nation reflects that; the opposite is true also. In *Rebuilding America,* if what is stated here is emphasized by church leaders, the aforementioned will occur. This book contains the best way—albeit long term—for the Church to positively influence and impact the State.

**US Congressman Scott Garrett**
New Jersey, 5th District

# Praise for *Rebuilding America*

In *Rebuilding America*, Ralph Drollinger makes a compelling case for the pressing mission of reaching our nation's political leaders—both at the state and national levels—with the transformative news of the Gospel. Ralph's ministry has encouraged my personal spiritual life, and I pray this book will help spark a movement to restore our nation.

US CONGRESSWOMAN MICHELE BACHMANN
Minnesota, 6th District

*Rebuilding America* challenges church leaders to begin discipling government leaders. That is what my good friend Ralph Drollinger means when he says "first things first." One of the tangential results is this: The Members Bible Study Ralph Drollinger teaches on Capitol Hill gives members of Congress a core, theological foundation derived from an in-depth, exegetical analysis of Scripture itself by which to weigh and measure the critical policy issues and decisions they face in Congress. It is next to impossible to build or rebuild any nation without this necessary component.

US CONGRESSMAN TRENT FRANKS
Arizona, 8th District

*Rebuilding America* takes the reader on an insightful overview of the Bible's teachings and examples of the importance of ministering to "kings and those who are in authority" (1 Timothy 2:1-4). Drollinger serves as a kind of tour guide as we journey through Scriptures from Genesis to Revelation, and from Abraham to the millennial kingdom, pointing out the many instances in which God's people both prayed for and witnessed to the political leaders of the nations. In short, *Rebuilding America* is a much needed wake-up call for all of us to place our evangelistic and discipleship efforts "first of all" where the Bible places them.

LARRY PETTEGREW, TH.D.
Provost, Shepherds Theological Seminary,
Cary, No. Carolina

# Praise for Rebuilding America

This is a small book with a large and powerful message. The central focus of this significant volume may surprise you and will certainly bless you. The Lord has given Ralph Drollinger unusual insights to an often ignored, cutting edge approach to advancing the good news of the Gospel. This is a book you will not want to miss!

DR. PAUL CEDAR
Chairman, Mission America Coalition,
Palm Desert, California

It has been said that if the Apostle Paul were alive today, he would travel to Washington, DC, our nation's political capital, and to New York City, our nation's cultural capital, in order to make disciples for Christ. In an age when many Christians have written off any type of involvement with politics, here comes a welcome update of Ralph Drollinger's book, *Rebuilding America*. This book demonstrates the need for Christians to present Christ everywhere, even in Washington, DC.

JERRY NEWCOMBE, D.MIN.
Christian author, TV-producer, columnist, radio host,
Truth-in-Action Ministries, South Florida

In an era of heated political debate that often includes deep-seated personal animosity, *Rebuilding America* provides a fresh, and much needed, wind of grace and truth. My friend, Ralph Drollinger, has challenged us to keep first things first by engaging community and national leaders for the sake of the Gospel, not simply our political agendas. I am eager to see how the landscape of the church's political involvement will shift as more followers of Christ engage our leaders with Christ-like tranquility, quietness, godliness, and dignity! Ralph is right. Only when this shift occurs will we see God rebuild America!

SHAWN THORNTON
Senior Pastor, Calvary Community Church,
Westlake Village, California; Bible Teacher, All Things New Radio

# Praise for Rebuilding America

Drollinger makes a compelling Biblical case for why it should be a priority for Christians to evangelize those in public office. Anyone truly concerned about transforming America should read this book.           BRAD DACUS
President, Pacific Justice Institute, California

Citizenship is one of our God-given Christian responsibilities. Drollinger has given us a clear blueprint to effective American citizenship when he urges us to prioritize sharing Christ with leaders in government, not because their souls are more precious than others, but rather because they have enhanced influence to share Christ with others and to affect government policy. And he supports his contention with numerous Biblical examples and citation, often using the original languages to clarify his message.

Those who wish to be "salt and light" in the world will benefit greatly from Pastor Drollinger's *Rebuilding America*.           JOHN A. EIDSMOE
Colonel (MS), Mississippi State Guard
Senior Counsel, Foundation for Moral Law, Alabama
Pastor, Association of Free Lutheran Congregations

While it may be politically correct for Christians to remain quiet and subdued in regard to reaching government officials, it is not Biblically correct.

Ralph Drollinger, in his book *Rebuilding America*, provides a Scripture-based strategy for every follower of Christ. I wish every pastor and every person who cared about America would read this timely message. Will you engage and will you accept your God-given assignment to be disciple-makers of local and national political leaders?
DUDLEY C. RUTHERFORD
Senior Pastor, Shepherd of the Hills Churches, California

# Praise for *Rebuilding America*

In the mid 1970s, there were concerted attempts to get believers and churches involved in government in order to change the trajectory of our nation, yet our national direction continued to spiral downward. Could it be that instead of focusing on the inanimate institution of government, we should rather have focused on evangelizing and discipling the hearts of our leaders? Drollinger makes a powerful, exegetically based argument for this adjustment in our thinking, and provides a plan to birth 1,000s of new ministries in city and county governments nationwide to bring health back to our nation. This is the same truth affirmed long ago by William Penn, the founder of government in Pennsylvania, who acknowledged that it is good hearts that produce good laws and bring good government.

— DAVID BARTON
Founder and President, WallBuilders

As a student of God's Word, I learned that New Testament saints were charged to carry the name of Jesus to all peoples, including governmental leaders. As a pastor, I saw our church impact our community and state by reaching elected and appointed governmental leaders. Now I am privileged to join my friend Ralph Drollinger as I lead the cooperative work of the 450 churches of the Northwest Baptist Convention to actively engage Public Servants with the Gospel and Biblical exposition. We need to be developing up-and-coming Public Servants for Christ everywhere!

— RANDY ADAMS
Exec. Dir.-Treas., Northwest Baptist Convention

# REBUILDING AMERICA

## The Biblical Blueprint

### Ralph Drollinger

CAPITOL
ministries®

Nordskog
Publishing inc.

Rebuilding America: The Biblical Blueprint
by Ralph Drollinger

Copyright © 2012 by Ralph Drollinger
Second Edition, Copyright © 2016

ISBN (Paperback): 978-0-9903774-4-3

ISBN (Hardback): 978-0-9903774-5-0

Library of Congress Control Number: 2016901692

Manuscript Copyeditor: Deborah Mendenhall
Editor and Production: Desta Garrett
Original Illustrations by Aude Cabaldon, audesign

All Scripture quotations are from the NASB unless otherwise noted.
New American Standard Bible® (NASB), Copyright © 1960, 1962, 1963, 1968,
1971, 1972, 1973, 1975, 1977, 1995 by The Lockman Foundation.
Used by permission.

Scripture quotations marked (NKJV) are from The Holy Bible,
New King James Version® Copyright © 1982 by Thomas Nelson, Inc.
Used by permission.

Scripture quotations in the Publisher's Word and the Map on page 24 are
from The Founders Bible: The Origin of the Dream of Freedom, NASB,
Signature Historian David Barton of WallBuilders; Brad Cummings and
Lance Wubbels, Editors. Newbury Park, CA: Shiloh Road Publishers, LLC, 2012.
Used by permission.

Printed in the United States of America
by BANG Printing

Published in 2016 for  by

Nordskog Publishing, Inc.
2716 Sailor Avenue, Ventura, California 93001, USA
1-805-642-2070 • 1-805-276-5129

www.NordskogPublishing.com

CHRISTIAN SMALL
PUBLISHERS ASSOCIATION

# TABLE OF CONTENTS

~

## APPENDICES

# INTRODUCTION

When we think about the subject of restoring a nation, what immediately comes to mind for many is 2 Chronicles 7:14:

> *[If]…My people who are called by My name humble themselves and pray, and seek My face and turn from their wicked ways, then I will hear from heaven, will forgive their sin, and will heal their land.*

This promise however was given specifically to the Old Testament nation of Israel. It is questionable whether this is a promise to believers in other nations today. Don't get me wrong, it is a good thing for believers to pray, humble themselves, and turn from their wicked ways. But is this a patent formula for restoring any other nation, like America? The promise is given only to Old Testament Israel, and it is not repeated in the New Testament.

1

So if the promise of 2 Chronicles 7:14 is not meant for us, does Scripture give us any other timeless principle for restoring a nation?

The answer is yes: Scripture *does* speak to the issue, and there is a prescription that equates to a timeless principle, not discussed much amongst earnest followers of Christ. Restoring a nation is difficult without a Biblically-informed strategy. In the pages that follow, I offer one such strategy for your consideration.

# CHAPTER ONE

~

# Paralleling America's Sports Ministry Movement

In 1996, my wife and I began Capitol Ministries.® This book, titled *Rebuilding America: The Biblical Blueprint,* is intended not only to explain God's strategy for rebuilding a nation but to simultaneously introduce the purpose of the ministry and the Biblical basis for it, as the two are one and the same.

When we started Capitol Ministries® in the California Capitol back in 1996, we did so with a desire to parallel the ministry methodology I had previously learned in America's sports ministry movement. I had ministered in the athletic community for 22 years, the last five of which I gave leadership to the trade organization of 87 separate local and national sports ministries. The big idea of how to reach athletes and coaches for Christ was and still is to place full-time disciple-makers alongside High School, College,

3

and Professional athletes—locating disciple-makers on their respective campuses (likened to the historically-successful style of High School and College campus ministries). After its small beginnings in the 1950s, today there are hundreds of sports ministers representing dozens of fine organizations who reach thousands of Athletes for Christ every year! We praise God for the fruit He has borne in the sports world!

In a parallel sense, we began soon after starting the California Capitol ministry, to franchise from the California base with the goal of spawning ministries in all 50 US State Capitols, as well as in Washington, DC. The specific purpose then and now is not to lobby for Biblically-based legislation (as important as that is) but to reach legislators for Christ and build them up in the faith. It has been our experience that strong believers will vote right on the issues.

Around the year 2000, as I prepared my weekly Bible study for teaching and discipling political leaders in the California Capitol, I discovered a recurring theme within the Great Commission: Scripture is replete with illustrations, examples, and commands that serve to underscore the importance of winning governmental authorities for Christ.

Illumined and excited about the insight God had provided, we began referring to this Biblical basis for our ministry by various names, some of them rather forgettable. Eventually that Bible study, with added research, evolved into this book, *Rebuilding America: The Biblical Blueprint*. As you will see in the pages that follow, the Apostle Paul and others were very much aware of this most efficient way of reaching the world for Christ and to the unparalleled positive impact such a strategy could have on a nation. I believe this was the means by which in the first century they "turned the world upside down" (Acts 17:6b, NKJV) in such a relatively short period of time. May this book serve to unfold and illumine the way they thought— and challenge us to consider how we might better work to not only fulfill the Great Commission but simultaneously rebuild a nation.

Whereas a sports ministry movement is certain to have a positive impact on many, helping to generate a movement for Christ amongst governing authorities holds promise to change the direction of a whole country!

# CHAPTER TWO

~

# Coach John Wooden and First-Things-First

During my college days I had the awesome privilege of playing under one of the greatest basketball coaches of all time, John Wooden. It was a wonderful honor to have been on his last two national championship teams. Many books have been written accurately analyzing his success. But having played for him personally, here's how I see it: He won ten national championships in his last twelve years of coaching by following a very simple principle: He did "first-things-first." That is to say he did first what was most important before he did anything else. Year after year our teams precisely executed the most important, rudimentary disciplines of basketball better than other teams. In a sequential sense we focused first on what was most important; every day of practice

7

we concentrated on doing what was most important before giving attention to lesser things. What resulted was total domination in the world of college basketball. One could say we "turned the basketball world upside down!"

A good example of the First-Things-First principle was the way in which Coach Wooden conducted the opening day of practice: He invested the first hours of each season carefully and redundantly instructing his players how to properly put on their socks and lace their shoes! He not only urged, but demanded, that his players—first of all—execute the most basic elements of the sport so as to construct the strongest foundation possible in order to attain college basketball's NCAA championship.

As a matter of fact, I would become the first player in history to go to four straight NCAA Final-Four Tournaments (due to the fact that in my freshman year, freshmen became eligible to compete on the varsity).

In a similar sense the Book of Acts records how a small band of men—the Apostles—in very short order impacted the *whole world* during the season in which they lived, and as one Bible translation states in Acts 17:6, Jesus' followers "upset the world"! These were not elite leaders, but a small team of uneducated, common men. How did they orchestrate such a huge upset in such a short period of time? How did they reach the world with the Gospel so quickly? *Have you ever stopped to think about that?* How did these guys in a matter of several decades manage to fulfill the Great Commission and change the world beginning in the first century? There were no printing presses to produce large amounts of literature, no radio or TV, no internet or social media devices. So how were they able to saturate the world with the Gospel—changing lives, changing culture—and eventually changing the Roman Empire? Scripture provides the answer: Not only did they do it one soul at a time through a ministry of geometric evangelism and discipleship, but they did it *by concentrating on and impacting a particular genre of society.*

Like Coach Wooden, they executed "first-things-first." Notice 1 Timothy 2:1, 2, 4 in this light:

> *First of all, then, I urge that entreaties and prayers, petitions and thanksgivings, be made on behalf of all men, for kings and all who are in authority,... God our Savior... desires all men to be saved and to come to the knowledge of the truth.*

In this passage we find *Coach* Paul urging his team members (specifically Timothy, who is now pastoring the Church in Ephesus) to do first-things-first: To

9

pray evangelistically and evangelize (per vs. 4) not just "all men," but specifically "kings and all who are in authority."

Look at this passage more closely. Verse 1 begins, "First of all, then," or *parakalo oun proton* in the Greek. *Parakalo* is a compound word comprised of the preposition *para* and the verb *kaleo*. *Para* means "to come alongside" while *kaleo* means "to call." Together, *parakalo* is an emphatic verb that means (in its first-person tense) "I call you alongside." *Coach* Paul heightens his commanding voice by including the word *proton* which means "first of all," in order to stress the priority of what he is about to say. Importantly *proton* is used in the Greek language to signify first in importance versus first in sequence. More literally these opening words read, (my paraphrase): *Let me say first (in the sense of sequence) what you need to do first (in the sense of importance).* First-Things-First says Paul.

He wanted Timothy to keep up his past ministry emphasis of giving precedence to evangelism (undergirding evangelism with evangelistic praying) not only for all folks in general, but for "kings and those in authority." Concern for political leaders was not an afterthought in his game plan; rather it was a top priority and passion that ran the length and course of Paul's life after his conversion. Here uncovered is the underlying basis for the direction he took. *This main concern in his ministry was one of the most significant elements—if not the most significant element—that vastly differentiates first-century Church missions strategy from modern-day Church missions strategy.* It explains, I believe, why the former was so much more impactful than the later. Keep in mind that the first-century church fulfilled the Great Commission and changed the world to come in their generation, whereas we have not.

Why is reaching "kings and those who are in authority" so important? It goes without saying that political leaders are often the most influential people in a society. Not only do they possess enormous power, but their capital cities are usually located near the center of the state. Political leaders and political Capitols represent the hubs of power, influence, communications, and transportation, with influence reaching into the countryside. Winning leaders for Christ and planting churches in these focal points makes sense for the practical reason of greater efficiency, effectiveness, and impact on the nation as a whole.

CAPITOL
ministries®

# CHAPTER THREE

~

# *The Apostle Paul and First-Things-First*

Who was *Coach* Paul's coach? Who taught him to give primacy to reaching political leaders for Christ? Scripture provides the answer. The First-Things-First principle came from Jesus Himself; Paul discovered it during his dramatic, life-changing conversion on the road to Damascus.

In the Acts 9:15, Saul (Paul's prior name) was blinded by Jesus and instructed to go into the city and wait there. Jesus then sent His messenger, Ananias, to communicate to Saul what had happened to him, what this was all about. Ananias was initially afraid to go because Saul was well-known as a persecutor of Christians:

> *But the Lord said to him [Ananias], "Go, for he [Saul] is a chosen instrument of Mine, to*

13

*bear My name before the Gentiles and kings
and the sons of Israel;*

Soon after blinding Saul, the Lord revealed to Ananias the reason why: Saul was Jesus' foreordained "chosen instrument...to bear [Jesus'] name before the Gentiles *and kings* and the sons of Israel." Kings were one of the three "people-groups" articulated by Jesus to whom Saul was to go and proclaim Christ as the way of salvation. As we will see in the pages that follow, Saul did not take this instruction lightly; he would incorporate these three aspects of his calling into the general and specific focus of his ministry.

There were many cities in the Roman Empire that had not heard the Gospel. How then did Saul (now Paul—soon after his conversion his name would change) decide where he would next travel? There were many factors he must have deliberated along the way, but undoubtedly one consideration was the presence of political leaders—such a priority would be a matter of obedience to Jesus' previous commissioning. Indeed, following his Acts 9:15 calling, Paul traveled almost exclusively to capital cities, the cities of greatest influence.

Like Coach Wooden, Paul lived by the principle of First-Things-First. What resulted in the long-term was enormous success—nothing less than *turning the world upside down.*

Paul journeyed to the following capital cities, many wherein he started churches:

- Paphos (Acts 13:6) was the capital city of Cypress.

- Perga (Acts 13:13) was the capital city of Pamphilia.

- Pisidia Antioch (Acts 13:14) was the capital city of Southern Galatia.

- Iconium (Acts 13:51) was the capital city of Lyconia.

- Thessalonica (Acts 17:1) was the capital city of Macedonia.

- Athens (Acts 17:15) was the capital city of modern Greece.

- Corinth (Acts 18:1) was the capital city of Achaia.

- Ephesus (Acts 18:19) was the capital city of Proconsular Asia.

- Rome (Acts 19:21) was the Imperial Capital of The Roman Empire.

Paul pinpointed cities of influence on his three missionary journeys; as he traveled he ministered to Jews and Gentiles for sure, but the point here is this: *He was called specifically as well to evangelize kings.* It is this same missionary emphasis that he entrusted to Timothy—and ostensibly the future Church—as his personal ministry came to a close. And, it is this First-Things-First principle that Jesus intends for His Body of believers to carry out today.

# CHAPTER FOUR

~

# *The Governing Authorities Converted in Acts*

The primacy of winning governing leaders is vividly portrayed throughout the Book of Acts in yet another way: Of the thirteen individual conversions recorded by Luke in his narrative account of the start of the Church, at least seven of those people are politically-related. The common thread amongst the following converts is this: They are those "who are in authority" (1 Timothy 2:2).

- ~ The Ethiopian Eunuch (Acts 8:27) is converted. He is the Treasurer of Candice, the Queen of Ethiopia.

- ~ Cornelius the Centurion (Acts 10:17) is converted. He is a Roman military leader of 100 men.

∼ Blastus (Acts 12:20) is converted. He is the king's chamberlain (i.e., Treasurer).

∼ Sergius Paulus (Acts 13:7) is converted. He is a Roman Provincial Governor.

∼ The Philippian jailer (Acts 16:27-33) is converted. He is a trusted governmental official.

∼ Dionysius (Acts 17:34) is converted. He is one of the Areopagate Judges.

∼ Publius (Acts 28:7) is converted. He is the Governor of Malta.

This insight into whom they evangelized is powerful evidence as to their priorities in ministry.

# CHAPTER FIVE

# *Luke and First-Things-First*

To whom is Luke writing the Book of Acts? Like his Gospel account, he is penning his tome to "most excellent Theophilus" (cf. Acts 1:1; Luke 1:3). In that he calls him "most excellent" a title used to address governors (cf. Acts 23:26; 24:3; 26:25), it is evident that Luke is inscribing this account to and for the purpose of persuading this particular government official to come to faith in Christ.

This may explain why more than half of the individual conversions he includes in the Book of Acts involve politically-related people. Luke's purpose could be either to convey to Theophilus that other governmental leaders have come to Christ (intimating Theophilus should also) or to illustrate the fulfillment of Paul's calling in Acts 9:15. His work serves both purposes.

Since he wrote one-third of the words in the New Testament (Luke and Acts combined) for the purpose of persuading one political leader, it appears that Luke, too, grasped the God-given strategic importance of such an objective.

# CHAPTER SIX

~

# *Paul Goes to Rome*

Paul's Acts 9:15 commission informs why he so passionately desired to visit the Imperial Capital of Rome (and for that matter, why he wanted to travel as far as Spain). In Acts 23:11 the Lord makes yet another personal appearance to Paul and tells him the following:

> *Take courage; for as you have solemnly witnessed to My cause at Jerusalem, so you must witness at Rome also.*

The Apostle had longed to fellowship with the Church in the world's most powerful city (Romans 1:10-12), but the Acts 23 passage serves to suggest he had at least one other compelling reason to make the voyage: To fulfill his clear calling by Christ to evangelize Caesar! In Acts 27:23-24 an Angel of God (a messenger from Jesus) conveys this message to Paul. Soon after, in the midst of a terrible storm, with his ship apparently about to sink, Paul tells his shipmates,

> *For this very night an angel of the God to whom I belong and whom I serve stood before me, saying, "Do not be afraid, Paul; you must stand before Caesar; and behold, God has granted you all those who are sailing with you."*

Given what this passage says, there was no reason for Paul or the others aboard the ship to fret that they would sink due to the horrific storm that was pounding down upon them. Why? Because aboard the ship was divinely-destined cargo—a man with a calling who was obeying the marching orders of the Savior Himself! In more of a paraphrased translation, Paul was saying, "Relax shipmates! Nothing can sink this vessel—because I am aboard—and I have an appointment with the Emperor!" (There's no reason to buy trip insurance when you travel with a guy like this!) Paul had a divine unction, a providential mission to take the Gospel to Caesar, and he knew that nothing could possibly stand in his way. Hand-picked by the Savior of the world who was the Lord of the storm, he would fulfill his destiny.

The Scriptures do not record the exchange between Paul and Caesar, nor does history record that Caesar was saved as a result of Paul's mission and ensuing witnessing efforts. Evidently, however, others in the Imperial Capital were! When Paul later pens a letter to the Church in Philippi (from and during his Roman imprisonment) he says in his closing remarks (Philippians 4:22):

> *All the saints greet you, especially those of Caesar's household.*

Caesar didn't repent but Paul had nonetheless been used by God supernaturally in the Imperial Palace. Here then is a man governed by obedience to the vivid memory of his arresting conversion, sobering commission, and specific calling. Are we as profoundly obedient as was Paul? How are we manifesting Jesus' commission to reach all of the capitals of the world for Christ?

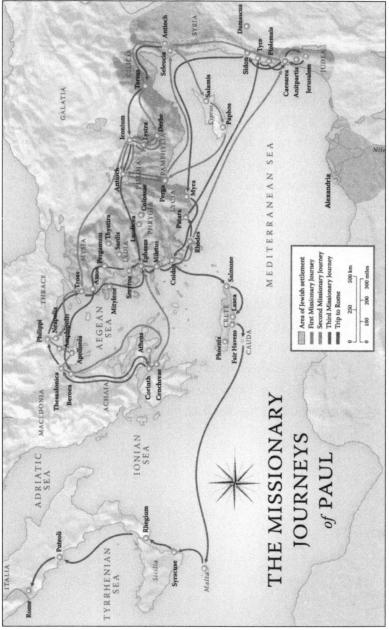

THE MISSIONARY JOURNEYS *of* PAUL

The Founders Bible, Newbury Park, CA: Shiloh Road, 2012, F-7.

# CHAPTER SEVEN

~

# Paul
# Goes to Spain

Given the formation, distillation, reiteration, and manifestation of Paul's deeply-seated calling, is it not reasonable to assume his intention to visit Spain had something to do with all this? It most certainly did. How is that? He desired to visit Spain after he visited Rome. This is observable from his earlier letter to the Church at Rome (Romans 15:23-24):

> *but now, with no further place for me in these regions, and since I have had for many years a longing to come to you whenever I go to Spain—for I hope to see you in passing, and to be helped on my way there by you, when I have first enjoyed your company for a while—*

Spain was a mineral-rich colony on the western-most edge of the Empire. It had a population of Jews and Gentiles who hadn't yet heard the Gospel. But of first importance, Spain was to the Roman Empire what Palm Springs is to America, an upscale retirement community for the wealthy—the rich and famous, powerful and influential; it was a community for the movers and shakers, the elite of Roman thought and culture. Spain was home for some of the most famous retired political leaders of the ancient world. The Roman emperors Trajan and Hadrian were both born and lived there. The orator Quintilian, the writer Martial, and the statesman Seneca all resided in Spain. Appropriately, as recorded by Clement of Rome (writing in A.D. 95, after the final penning of the New Testament), Paul eventually did reach Spain and "gave his testimony before the rulers."

Isn't that just so fitting for him! True to his calling the Apostle earnestly labored to impact all the political leaders of the world with the Gospel! (Lest you think I am reaching a bit when I say the above, notice what he said in the previously-cited verse, "…now, with *no further place* for me in these regions" [my emphasis].)

Paul possessed a deep-seated passion for the salvation of Rome's past and present political leaders. This heart of his, combined with the effectiveness of his strategy, informs us why he gave such an emphatic mandate to Timothy in the first-cited passage of this study: 1 Timothy 2:1-4. He was driven to reach leaders for Christ!

*Coach* Paul's missionary zeal played a large part in the Apostles' astonishing impact on the first-century world with the life-transforming truths of Salvation in Christ. This insight into their *game plan* serves to explain how they pulled off such an upset victory in a world dominated by the reigning champion known as "Greek Philosophy." Indeed, a rag-tag team known as *The Apostles* "upset the world" in the first century.

This upset is all the more astounding when you consider that the guys on Paul's team had little in the way of credentials; they weren't exactly Ivy-League intellectuals, nor even the sharpest knives in the drawer. But those apparent shortcomings were more than offset by their disciplined adherence to the First-Things-First game plan. In the end most church scholars today agree they fulfilled the Great Commission in the first century.

Their championship, however, was not rewarded by the outward possession of a gaudy, oversized ring presented in a hazy arena while fickle fans file out in contemplation of the next season. Rather, this team won an eternal, imperishable crown, a reward one day to be placed on their heads by none other than the Lord Himself. Not a league official, but God Himself

CAPITOL
ministries®

will someday say, "Well done, good and faithful servant" (Matthew 25:23, NKJV).

May each of us possess a similar passion—a quest for the same eternal championship that God has set before us: Encompassed by so great a cloud of witnesses, might we receive the upward prize of our calling and obtain an imperishable crown. *Think about that!* All else wanes in comparison! May we experience that same indescribable ecstasy by disciplining ourselves today to execute a similar game plan and receive the ultimate reward. Amen!

# CHAPTER EIGHT

~

# First-Things-First in the Old Testament

The consuming evangelistic fervor to herald the Gospel to "kings and those in authority" that encompassed Paul's life after his conversion is not enshrined with him exclusively. Expansively, this focus runs throughout the pages of Holy Writ from Genesis to Revelation. Let us now turn our attention to some of those passages which evidence this principle and perspective in other portions of Scripture. (Additional examples are also provided in Appendix 3).

In Old Testament times, Israel was meant to be a beacon of God's glory—to shine forth His goodness and salvation into all the other nations. More specifically, in order to accomplish this, she was called on *by* God to testify *of* God to the political leaders in all the other Gentile nations. The Psalmist best personifies Israel's priority of purpose in Psalm 119:46:

CAPITOL
ministries®

*I will also speak of Your testimonies before kings and shall not be ashamed.*

This mandate—to focus on reaching political leaders for Christ—is sadly missing in modern church methodology. Compare the near absence of present-day ministries aimed at reaching political leaders with the emphasis placed on such outreach within the following epochs of Biblical revelation. There are many organizations who, in the name of Christ, lobby for Biblical policy in the seats of government, but there are few who parallel what we'll see repeatedly elaborated on in the following pages of Biblical exposition. In other words, there is a discrepancy between what God's Word models by way of priority and what is presently emphasized in today's places of worship. Should there be any wonder as to why today's American church has been so largely ineffective in changing the direction of our nation? Returning to my metaphor, it's hard to *win* if you don't stick to the coach's game plan, and it's impossible to stick to the game plan if you don't even know it!

The following passages in the Old Testament serve to further build the case that evangelizing and discipling political leaders for Christ is near and dear to God's heart.

In the Book of Genesis God promised Abraham he would one day receive land, have numerous descendants, and be blessed (Genesis 12:1-3). Four centuries passed as Abraham's descendants expanded from one family to 12 tribes and then finally blossomed into a nation, the nation Israel. Why did the Lord call Abraham and his descendants out of the world? Exodus 19:5-6 states, My own possession," to be "a kingdom of priests and a holy nation"; "a people for His own possession" (Deuteronomy 4:20). Extrinsically, Israel was called to be God's special people—the envoys of Yahweh—in order to proclaim the excellencies of God to all the other nations.

In a *general* sense God intended for His people to become a light to the Gentile nations; and in a more *specific* sense He expected His people to be a light to the leaders of those nations. Notice in a *general* sense what God says through the Prophet Isaiah to Israel in Isaiah 60:3a:

*Nations will come to your light,*

Notice in a *specific* sense what God says through the Prophet Isaiah to Israel in Isaiah 60:3b:

*And kings to the brightness of your rising.*

The construction of this passage, from general to specific, parallels that of 1 Timothy 2:1-4: "…prayers …be made on behalf of all men [*general*], for kings and all who are in authority [*specific*].…"

CAPITOL
ministries®

Isaiah 49:6-7 uses the same type of general-to-specific construction regarding outreach:

> *He says, "…I will also make You a light of the nations so that My salvation may reach to the end of the earth." Thus says the LORD, the Redeemer of Israel and its Holy One, to the despised One, to the One abhorred by the nation, to the Servant of rulers, "Kings shall see and arise, Princes shall also bow down; because of the LORD who is faithful, the Holy One of Israel who has chosen You."*

Isaiah 62:1-2 further states:

> *For Zion's sake I will not keep silent, and for Jerusalem's sake I will not keep quiet, until her righteousness goes forth like brightness, and her salvation like a torch that is burning. The nations will see your righteousness, and all kings your glory; and you will be called by a new name which the mouth of the LORD will designate.*

The repeated general-to-specific outreach of these passages could be paraphrased: *Within the Great Commission exists the priority of reaching political leaders for Christ.* And I would go so far as to say that fulfilling this priority is the key not only to fulfilling the Great Commission, but to restoring a nation. Read on.

# CHAPTER NINE

# Solomon's Prayer of Dedication

The significance of God's Old Covenant saints laboring to evangelize Gentile politicians is also reflected in Solomon's prayer of dedication to commence and inaugurate the completion of the Temple. During his prayer, when Israel's King Solomon gave thanks to God (as recorded in 1 Kings 8:60), he reminded Israel that the Lord had blessed their nation for an outward, general purpose:

*[S]o that all the peoples of the earth may know
that the LORD is God; there is no one else.*

Solomon the architect had built the Temple with
God's guidance to include a very large courtyard
wherein the Gentiles were to come in and worship
God—all in keeping with the purpose of proclaiming
God's glory to the other nations of the world. As the
nations witnessed the radiant light of Israel, the hope
was that they would come from afar, led by their kings,
to worship the God of Israel. Isaiah 60:11 evidences
this idea:

> *And your gates will be open continually; they
> will not be closed day or night, so that men
> may bring to you the wealth of the nations,
> with their kings led in procession.*

God's desire here is plain to see: Israel was to be
about heralding Yahweh's glory to the other nations
(in general) and reaching their political leaders (in
specific). This was the holy purpose for including the
Temple courtyard in the overall design, and it explains
why the ultimate architect of the plaza, Jesus, would
in the future cleanse it from its detestable misuse on
two separate occasions. (See John 2:14-16 and Mark
11:15 respectively.)

First-Things-First in an Old Testament missions
sense meant that Israel was to emphasize reaching

political leaders for Christ as an integral part of the Great Commission.

Unfortunately, due to her disobedience, Israel largely failed in this ministry to win the foreign nations and their leaders. Instead of setting a shining example for the pagan nations, Israel's behavior was (for the most part) no better than theirs; the pagan nations were (for the most part) duly unimpressed.

When Israel did follow God's commandments, pagan nations and their rulers took notice. The Old Testament records several instances where kings came to "the brightness of [Israel's] rising." The following three chapters serve to illumine three of those occasions. (See Appendix 3 for additional Old Testament occurrences.)

# CHAPTER TEN

~

# The Queen
# of Sheba

The Queen of Sheba as recorded in 1 Kings 10:1-10 visited Jerusalem during the reign of King Solomon. The Queen had traveled a distance of 1,400 miles in a quest to satisfy her curiosity regarding all she had heard about ancient Jerusalem—Jerusalem at her apex was mesmeric in her bright splendor. The nation must have been extremely alluring because I can't imagine any classy lady (especially my wife) being willing to embark on what would amount to a 2,800 mile round trip atop a camel (from the location of modern-day Yemen) through a morass of endless, hot desert terrain! Scripture indicates, however, that it must have been worth it all; apparently she did not leave disappointed:

> *Now when the queen of Sheba heard about
> the fame of Solomon concerning the name of*

*the LORD, she came to test him with difficult questions. So she came to Jerusalem with a very large retinue, with camels carrying spices and very much gold and precious stones. When she came to Solomon, she spoke with him about all that was in her heart. Solomon answered all her questions; nothing was hidden from the king which he did not explain to her. When the queen of Sheba perceived all the wisdom of Solomon, the house that he had built, the food of his table, the seating of his servants, the attendance of his waiters and their attire, his cupbearers, and his stairway by which he went up to the house of the LORD, there was no more spirit in her. Then she said to the king, "It was a true report which I heard in my own land about your words and your wisdom. Nevertheless I did not believe the reports, until I came and my eyes had seen it. And behold, the half was not told me. You exceed in wisdom and prosperity the report which I heard. How blessed are your men, how blessed are these your servants who stand before you continually and hear your wisdom. Blessed be the LORD your God who delighted in you to set you on the throne of Israel; because the LORD loved Israel forever, therefore He made you king, to do justice and righteousness."*

Israel's glory affected the Gentile Queen exactly the way in which God had intended! She was overwhelmed and proceeded to praise the Lord. Luke 11:31 provides the conclusion to this wonderful story. During her visit, or perhaps resulting from her visit, she was converted! Israel's corporate testimony (at that time) proved quite compelling—the nation was in touch with God's script as to how best to evangelize foreign Gentile leaders!

**King Hezekiah**

# CHAPTER ELEVEN

~

# *The Babylonian Rulers*

The second instance of Israel's overwhelming national charisma is found after the reign of Solomon, during the reign of King Hezekiah. At some point in Hezekiah's rule political leaders from Babylon were enamored enough to pay a visit to Jerusalem. States 2 Chronicles 32:31:

> *Even in the matter of the envoys of the rulers of Babylon, who sent to him to inquire of the wonder that had happened in the land....*

Hezekiah too followed God's script, and the astonishment of Israel served to evoke the interest of the Babylonians to pay a special visit; whether they were converted remains unknown.

Unfortunately those are the only two corporate illustrations of Israel fulfilling her external calling

CAPITOL
ministries®

to reach Gentile political leaders in terms of them traveling to her. What follow, however, are perhaps the most powerful (of many, see Appendix 3) encounters between one of God's Prophets and a Gentile king relative to the proclamation of the good news of salvation and the impact that has on the restoration of a nation.

# CHAPTER TWELVE

# *The Prophet Jonah*

The final Old Testament illustration I have chosen to underscore Israel embracing the First-Things-First principle is the ministry of the Hebrew prophet Jonah. Though a reluctant minister, Jonah eventually (after one whale of a round-about journey!) reported to his assignment. He eventually got around to obeying God's call to proclaim His glory to the Gentile nation of Assyria, specifically, the capital city of Nineveh, most specifically, the king of that nation.

Of all the debauched countries in ancient history, Nineveh was a sewer of sin. For example, after conquering another nation, Nineveh would customarily skin the conquered king alive in the public square. In the Book of Isaiah the reader quickly notices that the Assyrians had a history of intimidating the nation of Israel. Certainly Jonah had good reasons to despise his prophetic assignment. The idea of preaching to that arrogant country with its despicable practices must have seemed not only foolhardy but impossible. "They will never repent!" But to his amazement the book bearing his name records that the nation did listen to his preaching; and soon Jonah had a specific audience with the king. Now himself transformed from a sideline ambassador of God, he is filled with courage, boldly calling the political leader to faith in Yahweh.

What followed provides an insight for those interested in the rebuilding of a nation: *Just as nations fall from within, they are turned around from within! Not only did the king listen, but he ordered the entire nation of Nineveh to repent along with him!* Jonah 3:3-9 states,

> *So Jonah arose and went to Nineveh according to the word of the LORD. Now Nineveh was an exceedingly great city, a three days' walk. Then Jonah began to go through the city one day's walk; and he*

*cried out and said, "Yet forty days and Nineveh will be overthrown." Then the people of Nineveh believed in God; and they called a fast and put on sackcloth from the greatest to the least of them. When the word reached the king of Nineveh, he arose from his throne, laid aside his robe from him, covered himself with sackcloth and sat on the ashes. He issued a proclamation and it said, "In Nineveh by the decree of the king and his nobles: Do not let man, beast, herd, or flock taste a thing. Do not let them eat or drink water. But both man and beast must be covered with sackcloth; and let men call on God earnestly that each may turn from his wicked way and from the violence which is in his hands. Who knows, God may turn and relent and withdraw His burning anger so that we will not perish."*

What a fascinating piece of history! What a compelling illustration of First-Things-First! Like Jonah of old, when the Church today emphasizes the priority of reaching political leaders within the Great Commission, it is possible, too, that a whole nation can be turned to God both efficiently and effectively!

Old Testament Israel understood God's principle of First-Things-First as represented by these four

CAPITOL
ministries®

previous insights: The design and inaugural prayer over the Temple Courtyard; the visit of the Queen of Sheba; the visit of the Babylonian Rulers; and the missionary journey of Jonah to a Gentile nation. All serve to illustrate that Israel understood (and at times embraced) the profound calling of God to proclaim the love of God to the political leaders of the world. May that be the case today in the Church! (Again, additional Old Testament illustrations can be found in Appendix 3.)

# CHAPTER THIRTEEN

# Jesus and His Disciples

To this point, we have gained from the life of Paul and the history of Old Testament Israel an excellent working understanding of God's laser-like focus on reaching governing authorities with His plan of salvation. Now moving forward from the Old Testament it is fascinating to trace this Biblical thread through other epochs of the Bible. With that in mind, allow me to work forward from Israel to the time of Christ, visit the Apostolic Period once again, and then journey into the future, i.e., the coming Tribulation Period and the Millennial Kingdom Period. Stay tuned— this all will amount to making my summary point!

When Jesus first commissioned His twelve disciples, He told them something very interesting in light of the thesis of this book. In Matthew 10:18, Jesus tells His disciples:

> *and you will even be brought before governors and kings for My sake, as a testimony to them and to the Gentiles.*

When Jesus first commissioned His disciples—even before He converted Saul in Acts 9—He expected His earlier trainees to reach out to political leaders as well. The New Testament importance of reaching political leaders for Christ does not start with Saul (later Paul) in Acts 9; it begins with the disciples in Matthew 10. Some might argue that being brought before governors and kings is a reference to the persecution many of them would suffer. But it is undeniable that many of them did reach out to those in authority, giving witness to political leaders about salvation in Jesus. Matthew 10 is the first chronological recording of Jesus commissioning and sending out His disciples. And so, in a precursor to Paul's instructions (in 1 Timothy 2:1-2), Jesus states here what is first and most important: Reach not only the masses, but the political leaders.

# CHAPTER FOURTEEN

# The
# Apostle Peter

One of the disciples commissioned in Matthew 10 by Jesus later elaborates more fully on the principle that Jesus bestowed on him, that Jesus bestowed on the others, and that Jesus would eventually bestow on Saul.

The Apostle Peter also had that Jesus-embedded aspiration to reach those in authority. Albeit Peter's heart to get a message to leaders is not as easy to ascertain from the Bible as are the others, the context of 1 Peter 2:13-14 studied in close proximity with the overarching thought presented in 1 Peter 2:12 (wherein

CAPITOL
ministries®

is explicated the main subject of the passage) strongly evidences his passion and zeal for "First-Things-First." What follows are these two Scriptures listed in reverse order (so as to more readily make the connection):

> *Submit yourselves for the Lord's sake to every human institution, whether to a king as the one in authority, or to governors as sent by him for the punishment of evildoers and the praise of those who do right.* (vv. 13-14)

By doing the above, you will...

> *Keep your behavior excellent among the Gentiles, so that in the thing in which they slander you as evildoers, they may because of your good deeds, as they observe them, glorify God in the day of visitation.* (v. 12)

In 1 Peter 2:12 (listed last, above), the Apostle is exhorting his Jewish-converts-to-Christ audience to live exemplary lives amongst the Gentiles rulers for a specific purpose: That they may as a result "glorify God in the day of visitation." This last clause is Peter's way in essence of saying that he desires that they be saved! Peter wants Gentiles and Gentile-governing authorities throughout the pagan Roman Empire to come to know Christ as is evidenced by the later portion of the passage (listed first, above).

This passage adds a great insight to the thesis of this book: The Apostle Peter explains the means by which political leaders best end up "glorifying God in the day of visitation": By believers—those witnessing to them—submitting to the laws of the same civil authorities! In essence he is saying that poor conduct in the Church will equate to a poor testimony in the community, and especially to the community leaders, the political authorities. Bad conduct, which includes ignoring or breaking the laws of the land—an evidenced lack of submission to governing authorities —would stand in the way of others coming to faith in Christ.

Simply stated, evangelism to Gentile kings and governors will prove effective only if believers humbly submit to the laws they enact (provided of course that these laws do not conflict with God's laws). In other words, if we want to provide a strong witness to political leaders, we must "keep [our] behavior excellent" and do "good deeds" while submitting to them.

Some years ago I was faced with a serious turning point in my ministry to governing leaders. I had discovered that some church leaders had been involved in, what I believed to be, unauthorized and improper access to personal computer data.

When I confronted them they ignored and down-played the intent and significance of the laws of the

CAPITOL
ministries®

land, using their institutional power instead to cover up their abuse.

As I grappled with this, I couldn't escape the import of 1 Peter 2: If I were going to have an ongoing, direct personal ministry to lawmakers—and maintain their respect as they "observed me," I realized I had no alternative but to uphold and stand for the laws of the land—even if it meant exposing the wrongdoing of these individuals.

I decided to stand on the principle of 1 Peter 2. To do otherwise would have adversely affected my ability to witness to political leaders (to say nothing of being complicit with what, in my opinion, may have been unlawful behavior).

When believers submit to the laws of the land, they "keep their behavior excellent"—which is key to maintaining a strong testimony.

1 Peter 2 serves as an additionally-insightful passage in this way: Not only is it stereophonic to the Apostle Paul in terms of underscoring the believers' need to be a witness to political leaders, but it instructs on *how* to be a witness to political leaders. This passage explains how a follower *of* Christ most effectively reaches political leaders *for* Christ. Be careful to submit to their authority (again, as long as what they demand is Biblical) if you expect to gain their audience.

# CHAPTER FIFTEEN

~

# The Future Tribulation Period

During the Olivet Discourse in Mark 13:7-9, Jesus taught on events that will unfold during the coming Tribulation Period. Wars will erupt, natural disasters will occur, and persecution will be common for all of Christ's followers.

> *When you hear of wars and rumors of wars, do not be frightened; those things must take place; but that is not yet the end. For nation will rise up against nation, and kingdom against kingdom; there will be earthquakes in various places; there will also be famines. These things are merely the beginning of birth pangs. But be on your guard; for they will deliver you to the courts, and you will be flogged in the synagogues, and you will*

*stand before governors and kings for My sake, as a testimony to them.*

Among the limited details Jesus provides regarding the Tribulation Period, interestingly He makes special mention of testifying to political leaders. In a parallel to His commissioning of the twelve in Matthew 10, Jesus states in Mark 13 that believers "will stand before governors and kings for My sake, as a testimony to them." Thus the principle of First-Things-First continues—even during this future epoch of great upheaval.*

Within the Great Commission exists the need to reach political leaders for Christ. This is a timeless principle that runs throughout all the periods of the Bible.

---

* Statements in chapter 15 and 16 more than suggest this author's premillennial understanding of eschatology. I realize there are other eschatological viewpoints, which if held by the reader, do not necessarily diminish the point being made.

# Chapter Sixteen

# The Millennial Kingdom Period

I am often amazed by the contempt that some believers nowadays show toward political leaders. Such attitudes run contrary to the respect *for the office* that is commanded of believers in 1 Peter 2 and Romans 13. While I am shocked by some Christians' disrespect for the office (though an attitude of disrespect is easy to come by when office holders continually conduct themselves in ways that are unconstitutional and/or less than Biblical), I must confess, when I see a surfeit of scorn and gossip, there is an element that I find a bit ironic. Let me explain.

Believers need to respect and learn from political leaders today because tomorrow every believer will become one!!

Subsequent to Christ's return,* God's people will

---

* See footnote on p. 54.

CAPITOL
ministries®

no longer minister to kings; they will *become* kings themselves! Many passages imply this: 2 Timothy 2:12; Revelation 5:10, 20:4, and 20:6. They are listed respectively below; notice as you read them the recurring word "reign":

> *If we endure, we will also reign with Him; If we deny Him, He also will deny us;*

> *You have made them to be a kingdom and priests to our God; and they will reign upon the earth.*

> *Then I saw thrones, and they sat on them, and judgment was given to them. And I saw the souls of those who had been beheaded because of their testimony of Jesus and because of the word of God, and those who had not worshiped the beast or his image, and had not received the mark on their forehead and on their hand; and they came to life and reigned with Christ for a thousand years.*

> *Blessed and holy is the one who has a part in the first resurrection; over these the second death has no power, but they will be priests of God and of Christ and will reign with Him for a thousand years.*

In the coming 1,000-year-long Millennial Kingdom, those who have been previously redeemed by
Christ will be given the privilege to rule with Him,
under Him, on earth. When Christ returns and
His Kingdom has come, He will grant believers the
governing positions similar to those who *now* hold
them—but unlike kings and rulers of today who are
subject to the Fall and sin, Jesus will be the ultimate
perfect civil ruler over all the earth. Believers will
then reign sinless in their glorified bodies under His
impeccable civil headship.

The English verb "reign" comes from the Greek verb
*basilius*. It is found in each of the foregoing passages.
This Greek verb stems from the same Greek noun
wherein we derive the English word "king." But even
though the verb and noun are very similar in Greek,
we do not say in English that "kings (noun) king
(verb)." Rather we say "kings reign" and thus English
Bible translators translate the Greek verb in that way.
A gardener may garden, a painter may paint, and a
driver may drive, but kings do not "king" in English.
Therefore when the above passages state repeatedly
that believers will someday king (reign) with Him, it
implies that we too will be governing authorities of
sorts under His perfect rule and authority.

If you are a believer reading this, get ready to
"king" in our future life! Such a position in society,

CAPITOL
ministries®

these passages indicate, is your destiny! So if for no other reason than personal hypocrisy, put away those bad attitudes you might possess toward politicians! (I say that and what follows in a tongue-in-cheek tone.) Should you not instead buddy-up to those politicians that you might so despise? You should, you know! If for no other reasons than to gain their skills to best fulfill your future job! On a more serious note, unlike them, Christian believers will someday (soon I hope) become the consummate, perfect governing authorities! Praise God!

In the future, the type of ministry every believer will possess toward governing authorities will radically change—from one of *pursuing* governing authorities *for* Christ to one of *being* a governing authority *with* Christ. Start readying yourself today, my friend!

These future-period passages serve once again to illuminate God's keen interest in governmental leaders. His interest remains intact even during the Millennial Kingdom.

# CHAPTER SEVENTEEN

~

# The National Benefit of First-Things-First

My New Testament Survey professor in Seminary, the humble, respected, and highly-published Dr. Robert Thomas, used to begin class each day by praying for the salvation of our country's political leaders. At that point in my life I hadn't yet discovered the truths I have just shared, and I asked him one day why he always prayed as he did. "It's simple," he said. "It's just a matter of obedience to 1 Timothy 2:1-4 where we are told to prioritize this." That made me all the more curious. And then he quoted 1 Timothy 2:3 from memory, "This (evangelistic prayer for political leaders) is good and acceptable in the sight of God our Savior." I now better understand what he meant; and I hope you do too. In that Paul first instructed Timothy to prioritize praying for the salvation of societies' political leaders, the same devotion to this principle should remain intact today. It follows that Christians and churches should not only desire, but engage in various outreaches and ministries to political leaders. Such is the Biblically-explicit, Biblically-based precedent of missions, promising multiple results.

I have held off to the last chapters to explain the here-and-now benefits of obedience to the First-Things-First principle.

God promises that if we will do First-Things-First, that is, obey Christ's command to evangelize political leaders, then something special will result. Notice 1 Timothy 2:2b—*right in the middle of this passage but often overlooked*—with this idea in mind:

> *...so that we may lead a tranquil and quiet life in all godliness and dignity.*

Hopefully you can now see why I spent so much time building the case for the prerequisite necessary to achieve the "so that," i.e., this magnificent result.

Is not "a tranquil and quiet life in all godliness and dignity" a good summation of what every American desires both personally and for our nation? Is that not the essence of the American Dream? *If so, then the preceding directive is God's formula for achieving such outward national blessings! Here is God's timeless prescription for building, maintaining, or restoring a nation!* Most previous and present Christian leaders have viewed and continue to view the Church's primary role as lobbying government relative to moral issues. This has its place and is necessary in a democratic republic such as ours. However, 1 Timothy 2:1-4 reveals the procedure—the Biblically-explicit formula—for Christians to *most effectively* impact their nation for good. It is First-Things-First.

What results from evangelizing and discipling governing authorities—*states the Word of God in this passage*—is a better nation, or in the case of America, in due time, a restored nation. *This is Scripture's cause-and-effect principle for nation-building!*

Scripture contains many cause-and-effect formulas. Notice for instance the simple construction of Jesus' Beatitude, "Blessed are those who hunger and thirst for righteousness, for they will be satisfied." In this case, satisfaction comes directly from pursuing righteousness. Satisfaction comes not from pursuing a goal directly, but as a by-product of pursuing something else. In a parallel sense, Scripture states that a nation characterized by tranquility in the citizenry results not from the pursuit of tranquility in the citizenry, but rather from prayers for governing authorities and the ongoing emphasis in the Church upon evangelizing and discipling those governing

CAPITOL
ministries®

authorities. Concentrating on this leads to "a tranquil and quiet life in all godliness and dignity."

One of America's Founding Fathers, William Penn, in the Preface to the Frame of Government of the Colony of Pennsylvania, 1682, led me to this truth: *Good hearts in lawmakers lead to good laws in society; whereas bad hearts in lawmakers lead to bad laws in society.*

Practically-speaking, executing First-Things-First impacts one's country for good because political leaders set the tone for a nation. It therefore follows that they need to have preferential treatment in Church missiology!

Believers must reach political leaders at all levels of their career paths if we are to rebuild our nation with a blueprint such as this. Not only do we need to reach state and federal governing authorities, but local and county political leaders as well. Such a strategy over time will generate the maximum effect and outcome. May God illumine these truths to our hearts and guide our steps accordingly in the days ahead.

# CHAPTER EIGHTEEN

~

# Tranquility, Quietness, Godliness, and Dignity

These four words chosen by Paul in 1 Timothy 2:2 are worth pondering, since, if for no other reason, they specifically identify the beneficial outcome both individually and corporately for having reached political leaders for Christ.

*Tranquil*: The Greek word Paul uses here is unique to the whole of the New Testament. It appears only in one other place in the Greek translation of the Hebrew Old Testament (the Septuagint) in Proverbs 14:30 which states: "A *tranquil* heart is life to the body,…" (emphasis added). Solomon's use of the word means "a healthy, sound mind and emotions" in contrast to his second stanza of the Proverb: "But passion is rottenness to the bones." The word used for "passion" is the same root from which we derive the English words "jealousy" and "ardor." Whereas internal tranquility results in external health, internal disruption destroys it. Accordingly Paul is saying that part of the benefit is physical health. In context, when one is fortunate enough to live in a country characterized by higher degrees of peace and serenity, free from continual mental agitation, living with a corporate sense of steadiness and stability, there will be greater physical health in the populace. These words are descriptive of the kind of place where you and I want to live and raise our families. Such, states 1 Timothy 2:2, result from evangelizing "kings and all who are in authority."

*Quiet*: I find it fascinating to plumb the Pauline use of this word. The same Greek root translated here as the English word *quiet* is also found in 1 Thessalonians 4:11 which states, "and to make it your ambition to lead a *quiet* life and attend to your own business and work with your hands..." (emphasis added). Paul's use of the Greek word *quiet* has similar, interesting and insightful *associations* in both this passage and the one to follow; the two passages contain almost synonymous attributes of what living a *quiet* life in the country actually equates to: It is not a stretch to say that his use of the word is associated and descriptive of the opportunity to pursue one's dreams, the freedom to build one's future via personal industry and initiative. Note in that regard this word is associated with "own business" and "own hands." Is it any wonder that where the Gospel has gone and affected governmental leadership and constitutional formation, that those countries have free enterprise and personal prosperity to the same degree that Christianity has taken hold in the leaders of the land? The two go hand-in-hand.

The second use of the word *quiet* appears in 2 Thessalonians 3:12: "Now such persons we command and exhort in the Lord Jesus Christ to work in *quiet* fashion and eat their own bread." Paul equates private ownership with his use of the word *quiet*. Again, context closely associates the Biblical word *quiet* with the idea of personal benefit from one's work and labor. This is in part the makings of a Biblical basis (theology) of capitalism versus socialism.

Lest anyone think this is a prescription for greed and selfishness, notice the remaining two words surrounding the first two that connote the benefits of personal physical health and private ownership:

*Godliness*: This word appears fifteen times in the New Testament and has the parallel meaning to "Christ-likeness." "What would Jesus do?" is a popular phrase defining what godliness is. When the citizens pursue personal holiness and the political leaders themselves have been affected by the same Gospel, the result will be a Christ-like culture of provision for the needy, care for the unborn and elderly, wise stewardship of the treasury, responsible development of natural resources into prosperity, and the list goes on.... Because the citizenry is godly, the culture subdues the earth, extracts its resources (by the sweat of their brow due to the Fall) with respect for the Creator's creation, and turns its God-given gift of raw materials into value-added beneficial products and services for the prosperity and well-being of all. That's how godly people in part manifest their *godliness* in the here-and-now. Evangelizing political leaders creates a Christ-like culture characterized by *godliness.*

*Dignity*: The repetitious use of this word and idea throughout God's Word carries with it in 1 Timothy 2:2 the contextual specificity that people have intrinsic worth, will seek to live honorably, will have seriousness in their pursuits, and will be compelled to move forth by the sheer gravity of their made-in-the-image-of-God character—in a world where political leaders and the citizenry are evangelized and understand God-imbued *dignity* as part and parcel of their being created in the image of God. *Dignity's* presupposition of freedom plays itself out in the form of a prosperous corporate citizenry.

These are the four benefits that Paul says will inure to a society—and to its individual members—when evangelism and discipleship of political leaders occurs! What wonderful results these are!

A very simple summary observation is in order. In the early days of the Republic, when our Founding Fathers were profoundly and forthrightly affected by their Christian faith, there was a higher degree of tranquility and quietness, godliness, and dignity (as defined above) than presently exists.

Why? The Church had purposely affected the Founding Fathers with The Faith. That infusion of faith fundamentally led to the creation of the greatest nation in history. Today the Church has shirked this priority of its mission, and the results are increasingly evident—look at what is resulting! American history itself illustrates this cause-and-effect relationship. The two go hand-in-hand; you can't have one without the other; First-Things-First.

# CHAPTER NINETEEN

~

# Conclusion
# and Application

The principle of First-Things-First implies that Christians need to emphasize reaching political leaders for Christ in order to best fulfill the Great Commission. This is how we restore our nation.

This brief study shows that there is great value, both presently and eternally, when believers focus on making disciples of political leaders throughout the world.

When the believer and the Church embrace reaching political leaders for Christ, there are at least three positive results: First, the believer is personally blessed for obeying a vital tenet of the Word of God ("This is good and acceptable in the sight of God...."); second, the Great Commission is efficiently fulfilled ("Who desires all men to be saved...."); and third, the restoration and preservation of the nation is gained ("so that we may lead a tranquil and quiet life...."). These three benefits are unmistakably evident from a close study of this passage.

May we partner together to reach political leaders for Christ in America and throughout the world respectively, for the praise of Christ, the salvation of souls, and the rebuilding of our nation.

By this point, I hope you are asking, "How can I become involved in helping to reach political leaders for Christ?"

A movement for Christ amongst our nation's political leaders will only occur to the degree we establish strong, fruitful ministries in the federal and state Capitols of our nation *and in addition, in the thousands of local city and county government offices throughout our land.* This much larger portion of the initiative is perhaps where you can best play a key role in God's mission; it can be achieved only by healthy Bible-believing churches taking up the cause of founding and building (for starters) weekly Bible studies in these public buildings. (Keep in mind that the supposed legal prohibitions against using public buildings for Bible studies have been consistently defeated in the courts; usually one only needs a sponsoring elected official to host a Bible study in a government building.)

For example, your church might want to cater a weekly lunch at City Hall or a county building or courthouse, and you could either help organize, host, or teach a Bible study for the building's staff and elected and appointed officials. This is just one of many creative ideas as to how believers can help reach political leaders for Christ. I am hereby issuing the call, and I hope we will soon see thousands of such ministries!

By stepping out in faith in this manner you will become acquainted with those in governmental leadership and therein establish a personal ministry, hopefully leading to their salvation and joining your local congregation! It is as simple as that if we are to rebuild our nation. Anything but this is to play an adult version of *Chutes and Ladders*.

Capitol Ministries® has specific training and Bible study materials available to you through our website www.capmin.org that are designed to serve and help you achieve new ministries in all your local and county seats of government. We call the outreach initiative of Capitol Ministries® that is aimed at serving, helping, and training you to develop ministries in city and county government "CivicReach.™" (See page 86.)

There are many other ways you can become involved in helping to reach political leaders for Christ. As the sports ministry movement has grown to become a part of American culture, the Body of Christ needs to found and maintain ministries to governmental leaders everywhere and at all levels of their career path. Together we can reach every elected official from the dog-catcher and librarian to the mayor and city and county officials throughout all of state and federal government with the Good News of new life in Christ! Where do you fit in?

Political careers can be likened to a baseball diamond. The school board or city council member has just begun his life as a public servant is on first-base

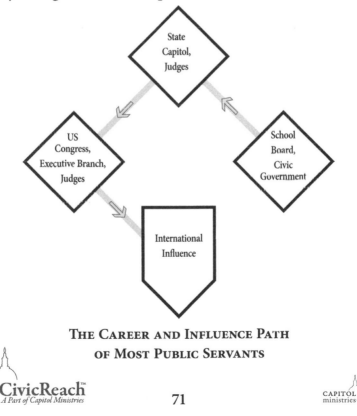

**THE CAREER AND INFLUENCE PATH OF MOST PUBLIC SERVANTS**

in his or her career path, whereas the US Senator is on third-base. Home plate is representative of obedience to the Great Commission, going into all the world to make disciples of the political leaders of foreign nations: mature in Christ US Congressmen and Senators are in the best positions of influence to win foreign political leaders to Christ. This diagram serves to pinpoint the various places and levels wherein believers can most effectively reach public servants for Christ.

How best can you evangelize and disciple "kings and those who are in authority?" Together we can reach governing officials at all points in their career path! Let us partner together today toward that end and by God's grace fuel a movement for Christ amongst our political leaders, not only in America but throughout the world! Amen!

# APPENDIX 1

~

# The Greek Construction of 1 Timothy 2:1-4

This inspired-by-God letter from The Apostle Paul to Timothy houses the main New Testament passage that buttresses the timeless principle of the "cause and effect" construction I have elaborated on throughout this book. If one reaches political leaders for Christ (First-Things-First), then the promised effect, in addition to others' salvation, is in the here-and-now: a changed nation. In order to more clearly capture the essence of this wonderful benefit, the following two critical observations of the passage are in order:

First is the need to clarify that verse four informs verse one. Verse four states what kind of prayers Paul had in mind: "who desires all men to be saved" is the context of *the prayers in verse one. Verse one prayers are to have an eye toward salvation. There is no getting*

CAPITOL
ministries®

*around the fact that Paul had evangelism in mind in these instructive passages. The relationship between verses one and four becomes even more evident when one considers the second clarification:*

An elementary principle of the Greek language needs to be stated: *The antecedents to Greek pronouns, if not a person previously listed, are typically the previous main verb, as opposed to a subordinate clause of the main verb.* Such is the case here in 1 Timothy 2:1-4 regarding the pronoun "This" at the beginning of verse 3:

> *First of all, then, I urge that entreaties and prayers, petitions and thanksgivings, be made on behalf of all men, 2 for kings and all who are in authority, so that we may lead a tranquil and quiet life in all godliness and dignity. 3 This is good and acceptable in the sight of God our Savior, 4 who desires all men to be saved and to come to the knowledge of the truth.*

The pronoun "this" at the beginning of verse 3 refers to the main verb in verse one (various kinds of evangelistic prayers) "being made." Why is this insight and explanation so important? It signals that what follows the word "This" in verse three is a further elaboration on the effect of (various kinds of evangelistic prayers) "being made." And what is that? That these kinds of prayers are "good and acceptable in the sight of God our Savior...."

That is to say what follows "This" is not a further elaboration on the preceding clause: "...in order that we may lead a tranquil and quiet life in all godliness and dignity." Again, the pronoun relates to the main verb, not a subordinate clause of the main verb.

What specifically is said to be "good and acceptable in the sight of God" relates to the main idea of the passage which is evangelistic outreach to others (in general) and those in authority (in specific).

Various kinds of evangelistic prayers (which are good in God's eyes) bring about the eternal effect of salvation (verse four) as well as the here-and-now effect of "a tranquil and quiet life in all godliness and dignity" in a given society. That's the point: Within this passage is revealed among other things, the formula that evangelism of leaders leads to the three results previously listed.

In order to better understand this emphasis of the passage, what follows for clarification is a rearrangement of the passage with "the-antecedent-of-the-pronoun-is-the-main verb (not the preceding clause)" insight in mind:

CAPITOL
ministries®

> *First of all, then, I urge that entreaties and*
> *prayers, petitions and thanksgivings, be*
> *made on behalf of all men, 2a for kings and*
> *all who are in authority, 3 This* [the cause of
> evangelism/prayers being made] *is good and*
> *acceptable in the sight of God our Savior, 4*
> *who desires all men to be saved and to come*
> *to the knowledge of the truth...2b so that*
> [the effect or result of evangelism / prayers]
> *we may lead a tranquil and quiet life in all*
> *godliness and dignity.*

The above construction serves to join together the main Pauline thoughts on prayer and to display the powerful "cause and effect" proposition of the passage more clearly for those of us reading it in English.

Stated differently, the construction of this passage reveals that in order to have a nation characterized by tranquility, we need to evangelize not only the citizenry, but those in authority.

These insights should create a better understanding of what Paul has said under the inspiration of the Holy Spirit as to the timeless Biblical principle formula for building, preserving, or restoring a nation.

# APPENDIX 2

~

# The Four Descriptive Motivational Words of Evangelistic Prayer

In 1 Timothy 2:1, Paul uses four words to elaborate on the specific kinds of evangelistic prayers to "be made on behalf of all men, for kings and all who are in authority" (vs. 2). The purpose of this appendix is to explain these words in greater detail with a view as to how they should motivate believers to seek the lost in prayer and outreach. Each of the words follows:

### Entreaties: *Deesis*

The Greek root word means "To lack, to be deprived." "To be without something." Its use in the context of prayer here and elsewhere throughout the Scriptures carries the idea of one's realization of the needs of the lost. The believer is to pray motivated by this fact, that God would supply the sinner the remedy for their sin via the Cross of Christ. The enormity

CAPITOL
ministries®

of the sinner's needs, that we are all sinners lacking and lost apart from the work of Christ on our behalf, should compel one to pray that God would touch each official with His grace and forgiveness and lead them to the way of salvation.

### Prayers: *Proseuche*

The only use of this Greek word in Scripture relates to prayers to God, connoting exclusive prayers of worship and reverence. The contextual idea is that evangelistic prayers, when the sinner is converted by the work of the Holy Spirit bringing him to trust in Christ, brings great glory to God. Hence we are motivated to pray evangelistic prayers because God is worshipped, reverenced, and glorified when He miraculously reaches down into the hardened soul of a sinner and bestows upon that person the wonderful gift of new life in Christ.

### Petitions (or Intercessions): *Enteuxis*

This Greek word appears only here and translated "prayer" in 1 Timothy 4:5 in all of the New Testament. It means "to fall in with someone." The idea here is that one gets involved in terms of understanding the sinner's plight. One does not pray for the lost with a cold, detached, mechanical attitude, but with love and concern regarding their future destiny.

### Thanksgiving: *Eucharista*

The believer is motivated to pray for the lost

because it is a great privilege granted to the believer by God. As ambassadors for Christ (2 Corinthians 5:20) every believer is given a role to play in the salvation of others. Exercising the privilege of leading another to Christ begins with thankfulness to God for the opportunity.

In summary, the believer is to go to God on behalf of "all men, for kings and all who are in authority" seeking their salvation motivated by these four facets of intimacy with God:

- We *entreat* Him because we are sensitive and in concert with the needs of the lost.

- We *pray* to Him and give Him glory because of His power to save.

- We *petition* Him because we are concerned for their future without Christ.

- We *thank* Him because we are grateful for the opportunity to witness on His behalf.

These are the specific aspects that should motivate believers to address God evangelistically, so as to achieve both the present and eternal results promised in 1 Timothy 2:1-4.

May these aspects of communion with God inspire us to continually pray with sobriety and diligence!

# APPENDIX 3

~

# Additional Passages Related to God's People Reaching Governing Authorities

There are many additional examples of God's called-out-ones who witness to God's glory throughout Scripture, and many additional accounts of God's ambassadors interfacing with kings and calling governing authorities to repentance. This book is not intended to be an exhaustive, comprehensive treatment of each of these instances; rather the format is designed to impart the First-Things-First vision and principle for missions via a quick, insightful overview. Following are additional passages accompanied by brief highlights of the respective reference. The pattern of God's ambassadors influencing kings is well illustrated by the sheer number of references that follow.

## Joseph and Pharaoh.

In Genesis 41:25, 28, and 32 the Egyptian Pharaoh asks Joseph to interpret his dreams. In the course of doing so, Joseph boldly states twice "God has told to Pharaoh what He is about to do" and "God will quickly bring it about." The Hebrew word for God which Joseph declares to Pharaoh is not the one used by Pharaoh to describe his pagan god. Rather Joseph uses the word "Elohim" the formal name of the God of Abraham, the one and only true God of the Bible. Importantly, Joseph is courageously "dissing" Pharaoh's pagan god in the preamble of his interpretation. Interestingly in this narrative passage, Pharaoh acknowledges Elohim with his own word choice (Genesis 41:39) and wisely appoints Joseph to run his empire. It would be a stretch, I think, to suggest this was an eternally-successful proselytizing encounter. Nonetheless Pharaoh's empire is profoundly influenced for good (Genesis 41:57) due to the ministry of Joseph in the life of the king.

God's appointed representative—who proved faithful, persevering, and diligent to minister to a pagan king—resulted in a more prosperous nation for all. This narrative passage is specifically and directly illustrative of the principle found in 1 Timothy 2:2, where, importantly, *the promise of national blessing is not predicated on the conversion of governing*

CAPITOL
ministries®

*authorities, but rather on the act of heralding the Glory of God to them.*

## Moses and Pharaoh.

In Exodus 4 God commissioned Moses to return to Egypt and stand before Pharaoh as His spokesman. Through the next 10 chapters Moses witnesses to Pharaoh regarding God's power, greatness, and ability to deliver. God's servant is empowered and bold. Unfortunately for Pharaoh and Egypt, Pharaoh is patently intransigent and unfaithful. Both Joseph's and Moses' separate accounts serve to illustrate how two nations are powerfully impacted via the faithfulness of God's people interfacing with those who are in authority (cf. Exodus 9:16; Romans 9:17).

## Samuel and King Saul.

King Saul was an Israelite, but not an obedient one. In 1 Samuel 13:13 God's servant Samuel confronts Israel's first-ever civil leader and boldly informs him of his sinful ways while in office. The fact that God used His Prophet Samuel—and that Samuel was willing to be used to confront Israel's first national leader—serves to underscore the point of this book.

## Mordecai and King Xerxes.

Similar to Joseph, Mordecai becomes the second-in-command. He served over the entire Persian Empire under the Gentile King Ahasuerus (Xerxes). By God's doing, the King was attracted to his proven, godly character. There is no evidence of Xerxes' conversion, but this account in the Book of Esther (see 8:2) serves to depict the ordinariness of God's servants being emboldened and elevated by Him to witness His greatness to political authorities and to achieve His purposes through them.

### Daniel and King Nebuchadnezzar.

In the book of Daniel, Daniel serves as God's man to the Gentile Kings Nebuchadnezzar, Belshazzar, and Darius. Suffice to mention here within the whole of this glorious account of the life of Daniel, he leads King Nebuchadnezzar to faith in God per Daniel 4:34-37.

### John the Baptist and King Herod.

In Mark 6:18, John the Baptist boldly confronts the sin of King Herod. Mark 6:20 implies that this secular king found both the character and message of the Baptist appealing; nonetheless he eventually bowed to peer pressure and ordered John beheaded. Again, depicted here is a willingness at any cost to obediently represent the ways of God to a civil leader with an eye toward the destiny of his soul more than the correction of his policies. Even though it would take another 300 years, this was the day the Roman Empire began to be transformed by the power of the Gospel!

CAPITOL
ministries®

## Paul and King Agrippa.

In Acts 26 Paul presented not only his personal testimony but the Gospel message when he addressed the Roman ruler. The King's response is stated in verse 28, NKJV: "You almost persuade me to become a Christian." Not a respecter of persons, nor impartial, Paul pulls no punches here. He speaks with all due respect, but plainly and directly to this ruler. This additional account serves to once again indicate the consistency of God's people reaching out to governing authorities in order to proclaim His glory and the way of salvation.

These seven additional passages illustrate that God's Word is replete with the First-Things-First principle of missions.

# Scripture Index

CAPITOL
ministries®

# A WORD ABOUT CAPITOL MINISTRIES®

*Capitol Ministries®* is a missiological response to the Biblical mandate herein termed *Rebuilding America: The Biblical Blueprint*. Its nineteen-year initiative has been to found evangelism and discipleship ministries in cooperation with local churches in State and Federal Capitols throughout America and the world, and CivicReach™ to city and county governments. Capitol Ministries® welcomes your partnership in helping to reach governmental leaders for Christ.

To learn more, please contact Capitol Ministries® at www.capmin.org. Help spread the word! Additional copies of this book and multiple copies with quantity discount are available from Capitol Ministries.® Inquiries can be addressed to:

Capitol Ministries®
PO Box 22 22 22
Santa Clarita, California 91322.

CivicReach™
*A Part of Capitol Ministries*

# ABOUT
# THE
# AUTHOR

RALPH DROLLINGER is the founder and president of Capitol Ministries.® After starting a ministry in the California Capitol to governing authorities in 1996, the ministry has established similar evangelism and discipleship ministries in over forty of America's state capitols, as well as overseas in Latin America, Central America, French and English Africa, and Eurasia. In 2009, he and his wife, Danielle, founded Capitol Ministries® in Washington, DC, where he teaches the Members Bible Study in our nation's capitol and they minister to members of Congress including over a dozen Senators on a weekly basis. One can subscribe at no cost through www.capmin.org to the same weekly Bible studies he teaches on the Hill.

Ralph and Danielle are the Governmental Sphere Conveners of the US Lausanne Committee on World Evangelization, more commonly known as Mission America. Mission America is a consortium of many Evangelical ministries that, among numerous other initiatives, share the common objective of reaching all of America's Public Servants for Christ in the years ahead.

Third-generation Californians, Ralph and Danielle are empty-nesters and when not in Washington, DC, or traveling to build ministries in capitals overseas, or mountain climbing in the Sierra Nevada, they maintain their residence in Southern California.

~

## THE SPORTS CONNECTION

Ralph Drollinger, at seven-foot-one, played basketball for legendary coach John Wooden at UCLA and was the first player to go to four NCAA Final Four Tournaments. During both his junior and senior years, he was an Academic All-American, graduating with a degree in ecosystems. He earned his Master of Divinity degree from the Master's Seminary some years later.

Drollinger turned down several NBA opportunities to play with Athletics in Action, touring the world and preaching the Gospel during the halftimes of their games. After his basketball days, he served in sports ministry as the director of the trade organization of America's sports ministry movement called Sports Outreach America before starting Capitol Ministries® in 1996.

1975 UCLA BRUINS CHAMPIONSHIP; COACH WOODEN (1ST ROW
WITH THE BALL), RALPH DROLLINGER (TOP UPPER RIGHT)

# Tribute to Coach John Wooden
## The Peripatetic Professor
Washington, DC, June 24, 2010

Historically rooted in the classic western model of education
is collegiate athletics. In the quest to develop the body, soul,
and spirit of tomorrow's leaders, athletic competition was
originally (and still is) intended to facilitate a vital role in
character formation. In the context of that beautiful tradi-
tion, I have always viewed Coach Wooden more as Professor
Wooden—one of the staff members of the University—
whose primary objective was not to win championships but
to ready his students for tomorrow's America. Those are the
vibes I got from him when he recruited me.

CAPITOL
ministries®

Of all my Profs at UCLA, he was by far the pre-eminent, the patriarch. He had the largest classroom with the fewest students; and his class met every day, almost all year, every year. His class syllabus had two primary ingredients not in writing: *impeccability* and *non-negotiability*. One even had to wear a uniform, with shirt-tail niftily tucked in, in order to stand in the presence of the maestro. Hair must be combed and the face cleanly shaven. Don't even think about getting away with anything inside his Pavilion.

His balance of instruction was both firm and caring. Unbeknownst to me, he knew about my mother being in a very dangerous surgery, the timing of which happened to coincide with practice. To my surprise, he stopped practice, called the team into a huddle and told us with tearful, loving eyes that he had just received news that mom's surgery at the medical center was a complete success. Who wouldn't play their heart out for a man like that?

Most of the Profs were about a didactic transference of information, but Professor Wooden was a peripatetic tutor I liken to Jesus. After 18 months, Jesus transformed a handful of men into His disciples and these few "turned the world upside down" (Acts 17:6b, NKJV); the teams of my professor did the same. Why? Because he walked with me and he talked with me; Wooden was the consummate peripatetic professor. Through the metaphor of sport the master inculcated in the next generation the skill of living life. I am so indebted.

Asked, "What did Coach Wooden teach you about life?" my answer is plain, "What didn't he teach me about life!"

RALPH DROLLINGER
Academic All-American, played on
Coach Wooden's last championship team, 1975

# A Word from the Publisher

### FIRST-THINGS-FIRST: The Mission

*He has told you, O man, what is good;*
*And what does the Lord require of you*
*But to do justice, to love kindness,*
*And to walk humbly with your God?*
(Micah 6:8)

*"... [T]he propitious smiles of Heaven can never be expected on a nation that disregards the eternal rules of order and right which Heaven itself has ordained...."*
(President George Washington, 1789 Inaugural Address)[1]

This book is about First-Things-First. The fundamentals come first. The basics. The essentials.

First, we must acknowledge and repent of our sins, turning to Christ, embracing Him, and acknowledging He is our Lord and Master—of the universe and of our souls. And be empowered by the Holy Spirit to begin living a humble and honorable and obedient life of peace and joy and service to our King Jesus and to our brethren and neighbors.

> *And He said to him, "'You shall love the Lord your God with all your heart, and with all your soul, and with all your mind.'*
> *This is the great and foremost commandment.*

---

1 Quoted in *America's God and Country Encyclopedia of Quotations*, compiled by William J. Federer. [Hereafter, "Federer"] Coppell, TX: FAME Publishing Inc., 1994, 652, Endnote 54 on 824.

> *"The second is like it, 'YOU SHALL LOVE YOUR NEIGHBOR AS YOURSELF.' On these two command- ments depend the whole Law and Prophets."*
>
> (Matthew 22:37-40) [2]

> *Our Saviour's great rule, that we should love our neighbors as ourselves, is such a fundamental truth for the regulating of human society, that, by that alone, one might without difficulty determine all the cases and doubts in social morality.*
>
> (John Locke) [3]

> *That religion, or the duty which we owe to our Creator, and the manner of discharging it, can be directed only by reason and conviction, not by force or violence; and therefore all men are equally entitled to the free exercise of religion, according to the dictates of conscience; and that it is the mutual duty of all to practice Christian forbearance, love, and charity towards each other.* (Patrick Henry) [4]

After His resurrection from the grave (on Easter Sun- day) the very last words Jesus spoke to his eleven disciples on the mountain at Galilee was their (and our) Great Com- mission. We should heed these words and embrace them and His admonition to all of us:

> *"All authority has been given to Me in heaven and on earth.*
>
> *"Go therefore and make disciples of all the nations, baptizing them in the name of the Father and the Son and the Holy Spirit, teaching them to*

---

2 Publisher's Word Scripture quotes (unless otherwise noted) are all from The Founders Bible: The Origin of the Dream of Freedom, NASB, Signature Historian David Barton of Wallbuilders; Brad Cummings and Lance Wubbels, Editors. Newbury Park, CA: Shiloh Road Publishers, LLC, 2012.

3 Federer, 399. Endnote 133 on p. 781.

4 Federer, 288. Endnote 49 on p. 761

*observe all that I commanded you; and lo, I am*
*with you always, even to the end of the age."*
(Matthew 28:18b-20)

The Great Commission emphasizes not only evangelizing but discipling, and that this means not just individuals or communities but all nations for Christ. Discipleship includes training in Biblical laws and precepts and principles of individual and civil liberty—self- and civil government.

> *The highest glory of the American Revolution was*
> *this; it connected in one indissoluble bond the*
> *principles of civil government with the principles*
> *of Christianity.*      (Pres. John Quincy Adams)[5]

Yet America today has forgotten God and rebelled against Him and thus declined exponentially in recent generations. Christians have shirked their duty of evangelizing and discipling even in our very own precious nation due to neglect in our lives and families and Christian duties.

> *God who gave us life gave us liberty. And can the*
> *liberties of a nation be thought to be secure when*
> *we have removed their only firm basis, a conviction*
> *in the minds of the people that these liberties are of*
> *the Gift of God? That they are not to be violated but*
> *with His wrath? Indeed, I tremble for my country*
> *when I reflect that God is just; that His justice*
> *cannot sleep forever.*      (Thomas Jefferson) [6]

> *History fails to record a single precedent in which*
> *nations subject to moral decay have not passed into*
> *political and economic decline.*
> (General Douglas MacArthur)[7]

---

5 July 4, 1821. Federer, 18. Footnote 51, p. 715.

6 1781, in *Notes on the State of Virginia.* Federer, 323. Footnote 52, p.766.

7 After recapturing Seoul from behind enemy lines, to the Salvation

*... [T]he general diffusion of Christian knowledge hath a natural tendency to correct the morals of men, restrain their vices, and preserve the peace of society....* (Patriot Patrick Henry) [8]

*Rulers are "ministers to God" to the people "for good"; they are "revengers to execute upon him that doeth evil" (Romans 13:4). They are to be a terror not to good works but to the evil (Romans 13:3). Their laws are to be conformable to the laws of God.... Human laws, therefore, in order to be obeyed, must accord with the laws of God: for where they differ, God is to be obeyed rather than man (Acts 5:29).... How can an infidel, who fears not God nor believes His Word nor regards His law, be a minister of God for good? Would not such a man, if made a ruler, in all probability be a terror to good works and not to the evil?... Let us resolutely resolve that we will spare no exertions to elect such rulers as God shall approve. This, believe me, is the only course of relief and safety to our afflicted country. Under the rulers of no other character has any Christian nation ever flourished for any length of time. Under rulers of a different stamp, nations have always degenerated and been finally brought to desolation and ruin.* (Jedidiah Morse) [9]

Yet we can stem the tide—as we have many more Christians in America today than the unbelievers Jonah confronted

---

Army, December 12, 1951. http://freedomoutpost.com/2012/06/general-douglas-macarthur-on-the-state--of-nations/#jhhjfcR3tYftHqhQ.99.

8 From the Preamble to "A Bill Establishing a Provision for Teachers of the Christian Religion" submitted by Patrck Henry in the mid 1780s. http://www.firstfreedomproductions.com/library/documents.php.

9 Rev. Jedidiah Morse, *A Sermon, Delivered at Charlestown, July 23, 1812, the Day Appointed by the Governor and Council of Massachusetts, to Be Observed in Fasting and Prayer throughout the Commonwealth; in Consequence of a Declaration of War with Great Britain* (Charlestown, MA: Samuel Etheridge, 1812), 30-32.

in Nineveh—despite our great decline from God's favor in currently experiencing His remedial judgment, *if* we get back to fundamentals, basics, essentials and cry out to our Master in repentance, seeking His forgiveness, and do the First-Things-First. And Love the Lord with all our heart, mind, and soul, and love our neighbor as ourself. And pursue the *Biblical Blueprint* in the goal of *Rebuilding America*. This is our goal, this is our mandate, and our cry (like that of John Knox[10]), *Give us America or we die, Lord!*

In this valuable book, in a First-Things-First approach, Ralph Drollinger wisely relates the strategic manner and focus in which we can participate in advancing the Kingdom of God on earth to fulfill the Great Commission … starting here at home in America.

The author proposes—and he cites pertinent Bible Scripture showing this is a more Christ-centered mission—to focus on changing the hearts of public servants as the primary emphasis versus focusing on the laws they enact. This is his ministry's *Biblical Blueprint* for evangelism, discipleship, and reaching and teaching the leaders, the movers and shakers, the public servants in our nation in order to accelerate the worthy and vital mandate of *Rebuilding America*.

Let us join Ralph in this crucial battle for the soul of America! Together, with Bible study, prayer, perseverance, and thanksgiving, let us run the race for the glory of God!

**Gerald Christian Nordskog**
*February 22, 2016,*
*George Washington's Birthday*

---

10 John Knox the Scottish Reformer was a mighty man of prayer. Here is an example of how he prayed, "O Lord, give me Scotland, or I die !"

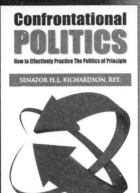